MY BOOK OF
100
BOOKS

CREATED BY ROSEANNA SUNLEY

BookReviews.RoseannaSunley.com
MyBookof100Books.com

ISBN: 9781793024091

Requests to publish work from this book should be sent to: me@roseannasunley.com

WHAT SHALL YOU
READ NEXT?

For book inspiration, visit...

MyBookof100Books.com

IMPORTANT!

I created this book to help you do more than simply achieve your reading goals.

Whether you read 5, 10, or even 100 books a year, it's all wasted time unless you implement what it is that you have learned.

I cannot stress how important it is for you to TAKE ACTION!

If you want to know how to do something - whether that be master social media, improve your leadership skills or start a business - there is a book out there telling you exactly what it is you need to do. Gaining knowledge on the subject will no doubt increase your chances of success, but ONLY if you put your new knowledge to good use.

The number of books you read is irrelevant...

...it's how many books you implement which really counts.

Roseanna

(I've never been good at motivational speeches, but you get the idea.)

The book number. (Make sure this number corresponds to the same number in the 'My 100 Books' section)

Pretty self-explanatory, add the book's title and author here.

53

TITLE: ....

AUTHOR: ....

ABOUT THE BOOK: ....
....
....
....
....
....

A brief overview of what the book is about.

DESIGN & LAYOUT: ★ ★ ★ ★ ★

READABILITY: ★ ★ ★ ★ ★

QUALITY OF INFO: ★ ★ ★ ★ ★

Use the stars to constructively rate the book. (I use the same criteria on my book blog and it works a treat!)

A simple way to quickly see how you felt about a book. Draw a smile, a frown, an angry or puzzled face – the choice is yours.

FAVE QUOTE(S): ....
....
....
....
....
....
....
....

I love quotes! Use this space to record your favorite quotes from the book.

I always scribble the odd note when I'm reading a book. Use this space to note your thoughts, ideas, and key page numbers whilst reading.

Lots of space with big lines for all your notes and scribbles to be kept in one place.

READING NOTES: ....

....

....

....

....

....

....

....

....

....

....

KEY TAKEAWAYS & THINGS TO IMPLEMENT: ....

....

....

....

....

....

....

....

....

....

....

....

....

....

....

....

List your key takeaways and things you want to implement in your work and day-to-day life. (You can use these notes to help you fill out the implementation section later on.)

"Everything you need to know has been written down somewhere."

ROSEANNA SUNLEY

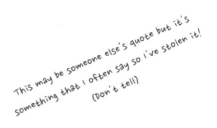
This may be someone else's quote but it's something that I often say so I've stolen it! (Don't tell)

MY...
100
BOOKS

...or in other words,

your book contents.

This number should match the book review number

1. ....

....

2. ....

....

3. ....

....

4. ....

....

5. ....

....

6. ....

....

7. ....

....

8. ....

....

9. ....

....

10. ....

....

11. ....
....

12. ....
....

13. ....
....

14. ....
....

15. ....
....

16. ....
....

17. ....
....

18. ....
....

19. ....
....

20. ....
....

21. ....
....

22. ....
....

23. ....
....

24. ....
....

25. ....
....

26. ....
....

27. ....
....

28. ....
....

29. ....
....

30. ....
....

31. ....
....

32. ....
....

33. ....
....

34. ....
....

35. ....
....

36. ....
....

37. ....
....

38. ....
....

39. ....
....

40. ....
....

41. ....
....

42. ....
....

43. ....
....

44. ....
....

45. ....
....

46. ....
....

47. ....
....

48. ....
....

49. ....
....

50. ....
....

51. ....
....

52. ....
....

53. ....
....

54. ....
....

55. ....
....

56. ....
....

57. ....
....

58. ....
....

59. ....
....

60. ....
....

61. ....

....

62. ....

....

63. ....

....

64. ....

....

65. ....

....

66. ....

....

67. ....

....

68. ....

....

69. ....

....

70. ....

....

71. ....
....

72. ....
....

73. ....
....

74. ....
....

75. ....
....

76. ....
....

77. ....
....

78. ....
....

79. ....
....

80. ....
....

81. ....

....

82. ....

....

83. ....

....

84. ....

....

85. ....

....

86. ....

....

87. ....

....

88. ....

....

89. ....

....

90. ....

....

91. ....
....

92. ....
....

93. ....
....

94. ....
....

95. ....
....

96. ....
....

97. ....
....

98. ....
....

99. ....
....

100. ....
....

1 TITLE: ....

AUTHOR: ....

ABOUT THE BOOK: ....
....
....
....
....
....

DESIGN & LAYOUT: ⭐⭐⭐⭐⭐

READABILITY: ⭐⭐⭐⭐⭐

QUALITY OF INFO: ⭐⭐⭐⭐⭐

FAVE QUOTE(S): ....
....
....
....
....
....
....
....

READING NOTES: ....

....

....

....

....

....

....

....

....

....

KEY TAKEAWAYS & THINGS TO IMPLEMENT: ....

....

....

....

....

....

....

....

....

....

2

TITLE: ....

AUTHOR: ....

ABOUT THE BOOK: ....
....
....
....
....
....

DESIGN & LAYOUT: ★★★★★

READABILITY: ★★★★★

QUALITY OF INFO: ★★★★★

FAVE QUOTE(S): ....
....
....
....
....
....
....
....

READING NOTES: ....

....

....

....

....

....

....

....

....

....

KEY TAKEAWAYS & THINGS TO IMPLEMENT: ....

....

....

....

....

....

....

....

....

....

....

....

3

TITLE: ....

AUTHOR: ....

ABOUT THE BOOK: ....
....
....
....
....
....

DESIGN & LAYOUT: ☆ ☆ ☆ ☆ ☆

READABILITY: ☆ ☆ ☆ ☆ ☆

QUALITY OF INFO: ☆ ☆ ☆ ☆ ☆

FAVE QUOTE(S): ....
....
....
....
....
....
....
....
....

READING NOTES: ....

....

....

....

....

....

....

....

....

....

KEY TAKEAWAYS & THINGS TO IMPLEMENT: ....

....

....

....

....

....

....

....

....

....

....

4

TITLE: ....

AUTHOR: ....

ABOUT THE BOOK: ....

....

....

....

....

....

DESIGN & LAYOUT: ★ ★ ★ ★ ★

READABILITY: ★ ★ ★ ★ ★

QUALITY OF INFO: ★ ★ ★ ★ ★

FAVE QUOTE(S): ....

....

....

....

....

....

....

....

READING NOTES: ....

....

....

....

....

....

....

....

....

....

KEY TAKEAWAYS & THINGS TO IMPLEMENT: ....

....

....

....

....

....

....

....

....

....

....

5

TITLE: ....

AUTHOR: ....

ABOUT THE BOOK: ....
....
....
....
....
....

DESIGN & LAYOUT: ★★★★★

READABILITY: ★★★★★

QUALITY OF INFO: ★★★★★

FAVE QUOTE(S): ....
....
....
....
....
....
....
....
....

READING NOTES: ....
....
....
....
....
....
....
....
....
....
....

KEY TAKEAWAYS & THINGS TO IMPLEMENT: ....
....
....
....
....
....
....
....
....
....
....

"The best investment you can make is in yourself."

WARREN BUFFETT

TOP 5 THINGS IMPLEMENTED

To help you stay focused on putting what you have learned into practice, list the top five things that you have implemented (along with the differences that they have made) from the previous five books you have read.

1. ....
....
....
....

2. ....
....
....
....

3. ....
....
....
....

4. ....
....
....
....

5. ....
....
....
....

6

TITLE: ....

AUTHOR: ....

ABOUT THE BOOK: ....
....
....
....
....
....

DESIGN & LAYOUT: ★★★★★

READABILITY: ★★★★★

QUALITY OF INFO: ★★★★★

FAVE QUOTE(S): ....
....
....
....
....
....
....
....

READING NOTES: ....
....
....
....
....
....
....
....
....
....
....

KEY TAKEAWAYS & THINGS TO IMPLEMENT: ....
....
....
....
....
....
....
....
....
....
....
....

7

TITLE: ....

AUTHOR: ....

ABOUT THE BOOK: ....
....
....
....
....
....

DESIGN & LAYOUT: ★ ★ ★ ★ ★

READABILITY: ★ ★ ★ ★ ★

QUALITY OF INFO: ★ ★ ★ ★ ★

FAVE QUOTE(S): ....
....
....
....
....
....
....
....

READING NOTES: ....
....
....
....
....
....
....
....
....
....

KEY TAKEAWAYS & THINGS TO IMPLEMENT: ....
....
....
....
....
....
....
....
....
....
....
....

8

TITLE: ....

AUTHOR: ....

ABOUT THE BOOK: ....
....
....
....
....
....

DESIGN & LAYOUT: ★★★★★

READABILITY: ★★★★★

QUALITY OF INFO: ★★★★★

FAVE QUOTE(S): ....
....
....
....
....
....
....
....
....

READING NOTES: ....

....

....

....

....

....

....

....

....

....

KEY TAKEAWAYS & THINGS TO IMPLEMENT: ....

....

....

....

....

....

....

....

....

....

....

9

TITLE: ....

AUTHOR: ....

ABOUT THE BOOK: ....
....
....
....
....
....

DESIGN & LAYOUT: ★★★★★

READABILITY: ★★★★★

QUALITY OF INFO: ★★★★★

FAVE QUOTE(S): ....
....
....
....
....
....
....
....

READING NOTES: ....

....

....

....

....

....

....

....

....

....

KEY TAKEAWAYS & THINGS TO IMPLEMENT: ....

....

....

....

....

....

....

....

....

....

....

10

TITLE: ....

AUTHOR: ....

ABOUT THE BOOK: ....
....
....
....
....
....

DESIGN & LAYOUT: ⭐⭐⭐⭐⭐

READABILITY: ⭐⭐⭐⭐⭐

QUALITY OF INFO: ⭐⭐⭐⭐⭐

FAVE QUOTE(S): ....
....
....
....
....
....
....
....
....

READING NOTES: ....

....

....

....

....

....

....

....

....

....

KEY TAKEAWAYS & THINGS TO IMPLEMENT: ....

....

....

....

....

....

....

....

....

....

....

"I don't divide the world into the weak and the strong, the successes and the failures...I divide the world into the learners and the non-learners."

BENJAMIN BARBER

TOP 5 THINGS IMPLEMENTED

To help you stay focused on putting what you have learned into practice, list the top five things that you have implemented (along with the differences that they have made) from the previous five books you have read.

1. ....
....
....
....

2. ....
....
....
....

3. ....
....
....
....

4. ....
....
....
....

5. ....
....
....
....

11

TITLE: ....

AUTHOR: ....

ABOUT THE BOOK: ....
....
....
....
....
....

DESIGN & LAYOUT: ★ ★ ★ ★ ★

READABILITY: ★ ★ ★ ★ ★

QUALITY OF INFO: ★ ★ ★ ★ ★

FAVE QUOTE(S): ....
....
....
....
....
....
....
....

READING NOTES: ....

....

....

....

....

....

....

....

....

....

KEY TAKEAWAYS & THINGS TO IMPLEMENT: ....

....

....

....

....

....

....

....

....

....

....

12

TITLE: ....

AUTHOR: ....

ABOUT THE BOOK: ....
....
....
....
....
....

DESIGN & LAYOUT: ★ ★ ★ ★ ★

READABILITY: ★ ★ ★ ★ ★

QUALITY OF INFO: ★ ★ ★ ★ ★

FAVE QUOTE(S): ....
....
....
....
....
....
....
....

READING NOTES: ....

....

....

....

....

....

....

....

....

....

KEY TAKEAWAYS & THINGS TO IMPLEMENT: ....

....

....

....

....

....

....

....

....

....

....

....

13

TITLE: ....

AUTHOR: ....

ABOUT THE BOOK: ....
....
....
....
....
....

DESIGN & LAYOUT: ★★★★★

READABILITY: ★★★★★

QUALITY OF INFO: ★★★★★

FAVE QUOTE(S): ....
....
....
....
....
....
....
....

READING NOTES: ....

....

....

....

....

....

....

....

....

....

KEY TAKEAWAYS & THINGS TO IMPLEMENT: ....

....

....

....

....

....

....

....

....

....

....

....

14

TITLE: ....

AUTHOR: ....

ABOUT THE BOOK: ....

....

....

....

....

....

DESIGN & LAYOUT: ★ ★ ★ ★ ★

READABILITY: ★ ★ ★ ★ ★

QUALITY OF INFO: ★ ★ ★ ★ ★

FAVE QUOTE(S): ....

....

....

....

....

....

....

....

READING NOTES: ....

....

....

....

....

....

....

....

....

....

....

KEY TAKEAWAYS & THINGS TO IMPLEMENT: ....

....

....

....

....

....

....

....

....

....

....

....

15

TITLE: ....

AUTHOR: ....

ABOUT THE BOOK: ....
....
....
....
....
....

DESIGN & LAYOUT: ⭐⭐⭐⭐⭐

READABILITY: ⭐⭐⭐⭐⭐

QUALITY OF INFO: ⭐⭐⭐⭐⭐

FAVE QUOTE(S): ....
....
....
....
....
....
....
....

READING NOTES: ....

....

....

....

....

....

....

....

....

....

KEY TAKEAWAYS & THINGS TO IMPLEMENT: ....

....

....

....

....

....

....

....

....

....

....

"Even if you're on the right track,
you'll get run over if you just
sit there."

WILL ROGERS

TOP 5 THINGS IMPLEMENTED

To help you stay focused on putting what you have learned into practice, list the top five things that you have implemented (along with the differences that they have made) from the previous five books you have read.

1. ....
....
....
....

2. ....
....
....
....

3. ....
....
....
....

4. ....
....
....
....

5. ....
....
....
....

16

TITLE: ....

AUTHOR: ....

ABOUT THE BOOK: ....
....
....
....
....
....

DESIGN & LAYOUT: ★★★★★

READABILITY: ★★★★★

QUALITY OF INFO: ★★★★★

FAVE QUOTE(S): ....
....
....
....
....
....
....
....

READING NOTES: ....

....

....

....

....

....

....

....

....

....

KEY TAKEAWAYS & THINGS TO IMPLEMENT: ....

....

....

....

....

....

....

....

....

....

....

....

17

TITLE: ....

AUTHOR: ....

ABOUT THE BOOK: ....
....
....
....
....
....

DESIGN & LAYOUT: ★★★★★

READABILITY: ★★★★★

QUALITY OF INFO: ★★★★★

FAVE QUOTE(S): ....
....
....
....
....
....
....
....

READING NOTES: ....

....

....

....

....

....

....

....

....

....

KEY TAKEAWAYS & THINGS TO IMPLEMENT: ....

....

....

....

....

....

....

....

....

....

....

18

TITLE: ....

AUTHOR: ....

ABOUT THE BOOK: ....
....
....
....
....
....

DESIGN & LAYOUT: ★ ★ ★ ★ ★

READABILITY: ★ ★ ★ ★ ★

QUALITY OF INFO: ★ ★ ★ ★ ★

FAVE QUOTE(S): ....
....
....
....
....
....
....
....

READING NOTES: ....
....
....
....
....
....
....
....
....
....

KEY TAKEAWAYS & THINGS TO IMPLEMENT: ....
....
....
....
....
....
....
....
....
....
....
....

19

TITLE: ....

AUTHOR: ....

ABOUT THE BOOK: ....
....
....
....
....
....

DESIGN & LAYOUT: ☆☆☆☆☆

READABILITY: ☆☆☆☆☆

QUALITY OF INFO: ☆☆☆☆☆

FAVE QUOTE(S): ....
....
....
....
....
....
....
....

READING NOTES: ....

....

....

....

....

....

....

....

....

....

KEY TAKEAWAYS & THINGS TO IMPLEMENT: ....

....

....

....

....

....

....

....

....

....

....

20

TITLE: ....

AUTHOR: ....

ABOUT THE BOOK: ....
....
....
....
....
....

DESIGN & LAYOUT: ☆ ☆ ☆ ☆ ☆

READABILITY: ☆ ☆ ☆ ☆ ☆

QUALITY OF INFO: ☆ ☆ ☆ ☆ ☆

FAVE QUOTE(S): ....
....
....
....
....
....
....
....

READING NOTES: ....

....

....

....

....

....

....

....

....

....

....

KEY TAKEAWAYS & THINGS TO IMPLEMENT: ....

....

....

....

....

....

....

....

....

....

....

"What we think, we become."

BUDDHA

TOP 5 THINGS IMPLEMENTED

To help you stay focused on putting what you have learned into practice, list the top five things that you have implemented (along with the differences that they have made) from the previous five books you have read.

1. ....
....
....
....

2. ....
....
....
....

3. ....
....
....
....

4. ....
....
....
....

5. ....
....
....
....

21

TITLE: ....

AUTHOR: ....

ABOUT THE BOOK: ....
....
....
....
....
....

DESIGN & LAYOUT: ⭐⭐⭐⭐⭐

READABILITY: ⭐⭐⭐⭐⭐

QUALITY OF INFO: ⭐⭐⭐⭐⭐

FAVE QUOTE(S): ....
....
....
....
....
....
....
....

READING NOTES: ....

....

....

....

....

....

....

....

....

....

KEY TAKEAWAYS & THINGS TO IMPLEMENT: ....

....

....

....

....

....

....

....

....

....

....

....

....

22

TITLE: ....

AUTHOR: ....

ABOUT THE BOOK: ....
....
....
....
....
....

DESIGN & LAYOUT: ★ ★ ★ ★ ★

READABILITY: ★ ★ ★ ★ ★

QUALITY OF INFO: ★ ★ ★ ★ ★

FAVE QUOTE(S): ....
....
....
....
....
....
....
....

READING NOTES: ....

....

....

....

....

....

....

....

....

....

KEY TAKEAWAYS & THINGS TO IMPLEMENT: ....

....

....

....

....

....

....

....

....

....

....

....

23

TITLE: ....

AUTHOR: ....

ABOUT THE BOOK: ....
....
....
....
....
....

DESIGN & LAYOUT: ★ ★ ★ ★ ★

READABILITY: ★ ★ ★ ★ ★

QUALITY OF INFO: ★ ★ ★ ★ ★

FAVE QUOTE(S): ....
....
....
....
....
....
....
....
....

READING NOTES: ....

....

....

....

....

....

....

....

....

....

KEY TAKEAWAYS & THINGS TO IMPLEMENT: ....

....

....

....

....

....

....

....

....

....

....

24   TITLE: ....

             AUTHOR: ....

ABOUT THE BOOK: ....

....

....

....

....

....

DESIGN & LAYOUT: ★ ★ ★ ★ ★

READABILITY: ★ ★ ★ ★ ★

QUALITY OF INFO: ★ ★ ★ ★ ★

FAVE QUOTE(S): ....

....

....

....

....

....

....

....

READING NOTES: ....
....
....
....
....
....
....
....
....
....

KEY TAKEAWAYS & THINGS TO IMPLEMENT: ....
....
....
....
....
....
....
....
....
....
....

25 TITLE: ....

AUTHOR: ....

ABOUT THE BOOK: ....
....
....
....
....
....

DESIGN & LAYOUT: ★ ★ ★ ★ ★

READABILITY: ★ ★ ★ ★ ★

QUALITY OF INFO: ★ ★ ★ ★ ★

FAVE QUOTE(S): ....
....
....
....
....
....
....
....

READING NOTES: ....

....

....

....

....

....

....

....

....

....

KEY TAKEAWAYS & THINGS TO IMPLEMENT: ....

....

....

....

....

....

....

....

....

....

....

....

....

"We are what we repeatedly do.
Excellence, therefore, is not an act,
but a habit."

ARISTOTLE

TOP 5 THINGS IMPLEMENTED

To help you stay focused on putting what you have learned into practice, list the top five things that you have implemented (along with the differences that they have made) from the previous five books you have read.

1. ....
....
....
....

2. ....
....
....
....

3. ....
....
....
....

4. ....
....
....
....

5. ....
....
....
....

26

TITLE: ....

AUTHOR: ....

ABOUT THE BOOK: ....
....
....
....
....
....

DESIGN & LAYOUT: ★★★★★

READABILITY: ★★★★★

QUALITY OF INFO: ★★★★★

FAVE QUOTE(S): ....
....
....
....
....
....
....
....

READING NOTES: ....

....

....

....

....

....

....

....

....

....

KEY TAKEAWAYS & THINGS TO IMPLEMENT: ....

....

....

....

....

....

....

....

....

....

....

....

27

TITLE: ....

AUTHOR: ....

ABOUT THE BOOK: ....
....
....
....
....
....

DESIGN & LAYOUT: ⭐ ⭐ ⭐ ⭐ ⭐

READABILITY: ⭐ ⭐ ⭐ ⭐ ⭐

QUALITY OF INFO: ⭐ ⭐ ⭐ ⭐ ⭐

FAVE QUOTE(S): ....
....
....
....
....
....
....
....

READING NOTES: ....

....

....

....

....

....

....

....

....

....

KEY TAKEAWAYS & THINGS TO IMPLEMENT: ....

....

....

....

....

....

....

....

....

....

....

28

TITLE: ....

AUTHOR: ....

ABOUT THE BOOK: ....
....
....
....
....
....

DESIGN & LAYOUT: ★ ★ ★ ★ ★

READABILITY: ★ ★ ★ ★ ★

QUALITY OF INFO: ★ ★ ★ ★ ★

FAVE QUOTE(S): ....
....
....
....
....
....
....
....

READING NOTES:

....
....
....
....
....
....
....
....
....
....

KEY TAKEAWAYS & THINGS TO IMPLEMENT:

....
....
....
....
....
....
....
....
....
....
....
....

29

TITLE: ....

AUTHOR: ....

ABOUT THE BOOK: ....
....
....
....
....
....

DESIGN & LAYOUT: ★ ★ ★ ★ ★

READABILITY: ★ ★ ★ ★ ★

QUALITY OF INFO: ★ ★ ★ ★ ★

FAVE QUOTE(S): ....
....
....
....
....
....
....
....

READING NOTES: ....
....
....
....
....
....
....
....
....
....
....

KEY TAKEAWAYS & THINGS TO IMPLEMENT: ....
....
....
....
....
....
....
....
....
....
....

30

TITLE: ....

AUTHOR: ....

ABOUT THE BOOK: ....
....
....
....
....
....
....

DESIGN & LAYOUT: ★ ★ ★ ★ ★

READABILITY: ★ ★ ★ ★ ★

QUALITY OF INFO: ★ ★ ★ ★ ★

FAVE QUOTE(S): ....
....
....
....
....
....
....
....

READING NOTES: ....

....

....

....

....

....

....

....

....

....

KEY TAKEAWAYS & THINGS TO IMPLEMENT: ....

....

....

....

....

....

....

....

....

....

....

"It is your attitude, not your aptitude, that determines your altitude."

ZIG ZIGLAR

TOP 5 THINGS IMPLEMENTED

To help you stay focused on putting what you have learned into practice, list the top five things that you have implemented (along with the differences that they have made) from the previous five books you have read.

1. ....
....
....
....

2. ....
....
....
....

3. ....
....
....
....

4. ....
....
....
....

5. ....
....
....
....

31

TITLE: ....

AUTHOR: ....

ABOUT THE BOOK: ....
....
....
....
....
....

DESIGN & LAYOUT: ★ ★ ★ ★ ★

READABILITY: ★ ★ ★ ★ ★

QUALITY OF INFO: ★ ★ ★ ★ ★

FAVE QUOTE(S): ....
....
....
....
....
....
....
....

READING NOTES: ....

....

....

....

....

....

....

....

....

....

KEY TAKEAWAYS & THINGS TO IMPLEMENT: ....

....

....

....

....

....

....

....

....

....

....

32

TITLE: ....

AUTHOR: ....

ABOUT THE BOOK: ....
....
....
....
....
....

DESIGN & LAYOUT: ⭐ ⭐ ⭐ ⭐ ⭐

READABILITY: ⭐ ⭐ ⭐ ⭐ ⭐

QUALITY OF INFO: ⭐ ⭐ ⭐ ⭐ ⭐

FAVE QUOTE(S): ....
....
....
....
....
....
....
....

READING NOTES: ....

....

....

....

....

....

....

....

....

....

KEY TAKEAWAYS & THINGS TO IMPLEMENT: ....

....

....

....

....

....

....

....

....

....

....

33 TITLE: ....

AUTHOR: ....

ABOUT THE BOOK: ....
....
....
....
....
....

DESIGN & LAYOUT: ★★★★★

READABILITY: ★★★★★

QUALITY OF INFO: ★★★★★

FAVE QUOTE(S): ....
....
....
....
....
....
....
....

READING NOTES: ....
....
....
....
....
....
....
....
....
....

KEY TAKEAWAYS & THINGS TO IMPLEMENT: ....
....
....
....
....
....
....
....
....
....
....
....

34 TITLE: ....

AUTHOR: ....

ABOUT THE BOOK: ....
....
....
....
....
....

DESIGN & LAYOUT: ★★★★★

READABILITY: ★★★★★

QUALITY OF INFO: ★★★★★

FAVE QUOTE(S): ....
....
....
....
....
....
....
....

READING NOTES: ....

....

....

....

....

....

....

....

....

....

KEY TAKEAWAYS & THINGS TO IMPLEMENT: ....

....

....

....

....

....

....

....

....

....

....

35

TITLE: ....

AUTHOR: ....

ABOUT THE BOOK: ....
....
....
....
....
....

DESIGN & LAYOUT: ★ ★ ★ ★ ★

READABILITY: ★ ★ ★ ★ ★

QUALITY OF INFO: ★ ★ ★ ★ ★

FAVE QUOTE(S): ....
....
....
....
....
....
....
....

READING NOTES: ....
....
....
....
....
....
....
....
....
....

KEY TAKEAWAYS & THINGS TO IMPLEMENT: ....
....
....
....
....
....
....
....
....
....
....

"It ain't what you know that gets you into trouble. It's what you know for sure that just ain't so."

MARK TWAIN

TOP 5 THINGS IMPLEMENTED

To help you stay focused on putting what you have learned into practice, list the top five things that you have implemented (along with the differences that they have made) from the previous five books you have read.

1. ....
....
....
....

2. ....
....
....
....

3. ....
....
....
....

4. ....
....
....
....

5. ....
....
....
....

36

TITLE: ....

AUTHOR: ....

ABOUT THE BOOK: ....
....
....
....
....
....

DESIGN & LAYOUT: ☆ ☆ ☆ ☆ ☆

READABILITY: ☆ ☆ ☆ ☆ ☆

QUALITY OF INFO: ☆ ☆ ☆ ☆ ☆

FAVE QUOTE(S): ....
....
....
....
....
....
....
....

READING NOTES: ....

....

....

....

....

....

....

....

....

....

....

KEY TAKEAWAYS & THINGS TO IMPLEMENT: ....

....

....

....

....

....

....

....

....

....

....

....

37

TITLE: ....

AUTHOR: ....

ABOUT THE BOOK: ....
....
....
....
....
....

DESIGN & LAYOUT: ★ ★ ★ ★ ★

READABILITY: ★ ★ ★ ★ ★

QUALITY OF INFO: ★ ★ ★ ★ ★

FAVE QUOTE(S): ....
....
....
....
....
....
....
....

READING NOTES: ....

....

....

....

....

....

....

....

....

....

KEY TAKEAWAYS & THINGS TO IMPLEMENT: ....

....

....

....

....

....

....

....

....

....

38

TITLE: ....

AUTHOR: ....

ABOUT THE BOOK: ....
....
....
....
....
....

DESIGN & LAYOUT: ★★★★★

READABILITY: ★★★★★

QUALITY OF INFO: ★★★★★

FAVE QUOTE(S): ....
....
....
....
....
....
....
....

READING NOTES: ....
....
....
....
....
....
....
....
....
....

KEY TAKEAWAYS & THINGS TO IMPLEMENT: ....
....
....
....
....
....
....
....
....
....
....

39

TITLE: ....

AUTHOR: ....

ABOUT THE BOOK: ....
....
....
....
....
....

DESIGN & LAYOUT: ★ ★ ★ ★ ★

READABILITY: ★ ★ ★ ★ ★

QUALITY OF INFO: ★ ★ ★ ★ ★

FAVE QUOTE(S): ....
....
....
....
....
....
....
....

READING NOTES: ....

....

....

....

....

....

....

....

....

....

KEY TAKEAWAYS & THINGS TO IMPLEMENT: ....

....

....

....

....

....

....

....

....

....

....

....

40

TITLE: ....

AUTHOR: ....

ABOUT THE BOOK: ....
....
....
....
....
....

DESIGN & LAYOUT: ★ ★ ★ ★ ★

READABILITY: ★ ★ ★ ★ ★

QUALITY OF INFO: ★ ★ ★ ★ ★

FAVE QUOTE(S): ....
....
....
....
....
....
....
....

READING NOTES: ....
....
....
....
....
....
....
....
....
....

KEY TAKEAWAYS & THINGS TO IMPLEMENT: ....
....
....
....
....
....
....
....
....
....
....

"Successful and unsuccessful people
do not vary greatly in their abilities.
They vary in their desire to
reach their potential."

JOHN MAXWELL

TOP 5 THINGS IMPLEMENTED

To help you stay focused on putting what you have learned into practice, list the top five things that you have implemented (along with the differences that they have made) from the previous five books you have read.

1. ....
....
....
....

2. ....
....
....
....

3. ....
....
....
....

4. ....
....
....
....

5. ....
....
....
....

41

TITLE: ....

AUTHOR: ....

ABOUT THE BOOK: ....
....
....
....
....
....

DESIGN & LAYOUT: ★ ★ ★ ★ ★

READABILITY: ★ ★ ★ ★ ★

QUALITY OF INFO: ★ ★ ★ ★ ★

FAVE QUOTE(S): ....
....
....
....
....
....
....
....

READING NOTES: ....

....

....

....

....

....

....

....

....

....

KEY TAKEAWAYS & THINGS TO IMPLEMENT: ....

....

....

....

....

....

....

....

....

....

....

42

TITLE: ....

AUTHOR: ....

ABOUT THE BOOK: ....
....
....
....
....
....

DESIGN & LAYOUT: ★★★★★

READABILITY: ★★★★★

QUALITY OF INFO: ★★★★★

FAVE QUOTE(S): ....
....
....
....
....
....
....
....

READING NOTES: ....

....

....

....

....

....

....

....

....

....

KEY TAKEAWAYS & THINGS TO IMPLEMENT: ....

....

....

....

....

....

....

....

....

....

....

43

TITLE: ....

AUTHOR: ....

ABOUT THE BOOK: ....
....
....
....
....
....

DESIGN & LAYOUT: ★ ★ ★ ★ ★

READABILITY: ★ ★ ★ ★ ★

QUALITY OF INFO: ★ ★ ★ ★ ★

FAVE QUOTE(S): ....
....
....
....
....
....
....
....

READING NOTES: ....

....

....

....

....

....

....

....

....

....

KEY TAKEAWAYS & THINGS TO IMPLEMENT: ....

....

....

....

....

....

....

....

....

....

....

....

44

TITLE: ....

AUTHOR: ....

ABOUT THE BOOK: ....
....
....
....
....
....

DESIGN & LAYOUT: ★ ★ ★ ★ ★

READABILITY: ★ ★ ★ ★ ★

QUALITY OF INFO: ★ ★ ★ ★ ★

FAVE QUOTE(S): ....
....
....
....
....
....
....
....

READING NOTES: ....

....

....

....

....

....

....

....

....

....

KEY TAKEAWAYS & THINGS TO IMPLEMENT: ....

....

....

....

....

....

....

....

....

....

....

45

TITLE: ....

AUTHOR: ....

ABOUT THE BOOK: ....
....
....
....
....
....

DESIGN & LAYOUT: ★★★★★

READABILITY: ★★★★★

QUALITY OF INFO: ★★★★★

FAVE QUOTE(S): ....
....
....
....
....
....
....
....

READING NOTES: ....

....

....

....

....

....

....

....

....

....

KEY TAKEAWAYS & THINGS TO IMPLEMENT: ....

....

....

....

....

....

....

....

....

....

....

"People do not decide their futures,
they decide their habits and
their habits decide their futures."

SHEL SILVERSTEIN

TOP 5 THINGS IMPLEMENTED

To help you stay focused on putting what you have learned into practice, list the top five things that you have implemented (along with the differences that they have made) from the previous five books you have read.

1. ....
....
....
....

2. ....
....
....
....

3. ....
....
....
....

4. ....
....
....
....

5. ....
....
....
....

46

TITLE: ....

AUTHOR: ....

ABOUT THE BOOK: ....
....
....
....
....
....

DESIGN & LAYOUT: ★ ★ ★ ★ ★

READABILITY: ★ ★ ★ ★ ★

QUALITY OF INFO: ★ ★ ★ ★ ★

FAVE QUOTE(S): ....
....
....
....
....
....
....
....

READING NOTES: ....
....
....
....
....
....
....
....
....
....
....

KEY TAKEAWAYS & THINGS TO IMPLEMENT: ....
....
....
....
....
....
....
....
....
....
....
....
....

47

TITLE: ....

AUTHOR: ....

ABOUT THE BOOK: ....
....
....
....
....
....

DESIGN & LAYOUT: ★ ★ ★ ★ ★

READABILITY: ★ ★ ★ ★ ★

QUALITY OF INFO: ★ ★ ★ ★ ★

FAVE QUOTE(S): ....
....
....
....
....
....
....
....

READING NOTES: ....

....

....

....

....

....

....

....

....

....

KEY TAKEAWAYS & THINGS TO IMPLEMENT: ....

....

....

....

....

....

....

....

....

....

....

48

TITLE: ....

AUTHOR: ....

ABOUT THE BOOK: ....
....
....
....
....
....

DESIGN & LAYOUT: ★ ★ ★ ★ ★

READABILITY: ★ ★ ★ ★ ★

QUALITY OF INFO: ★ ★ ★ ★ ★

FAVE QUOTE(S): ....
....
....
....
....
....
....
....

READING NOTES: ....
....
....
....
....
....
....
....
....
....
....

KEY TAKEAWAYS & THINGS TO IMPLEMENT: ....
....
....
....
....
....
....
....
....
....
....
....

49 TITLE: ....

AUTHOR: ....

ABOUT THE BOOK: ....
....
....
....
....
....

DESIGN & LAYOUT: ★ ★ ★ ★ ★

READABILITY: ★ ★ ★ ★ ★

QUALITY OF INFO: ★ ★ ★ ★ ★

FAVE QUOTE(S): ....
....
....
....
....
....
....
....

READING NOTES: ....

....

....

....

....

....

....

....

....

....

KEY TAKEAWAYS & THINGS TO IMPLEMENT: ....

....

....

....

....

....

....

....

....

....

....

50

TITLE: ....

AUTHOR: ....

ABOUT THE BOOK: ....
....
....
....
....
....

DESIGN & LAYOUT: ⭐ ⭐ ⭐ ⭐ ⭐

READABILITY: ⭐ ⭐ ⭐ ⭐ ⭐

QUALITY OF INFO: ⭐ ⭐ ⭐ ⭐ ⭐

FAVE QUOTE(S): ....
....
....
....
....
....
....
....

READING NOTES: ....

....

....

....

....

....

....

....

....

....

KEY TAKEAWAYS & THINGS TO IMPLEMENT: ....

....

....

....

....

....

....

....

....

....

....

"Striving for success without hard work
is like trying to harvest where
you haven't planted."

DAVID BLY

TOP 5 THINGS IMPLEMENTED

To help you stay focused on putting what you have learned into practice, list the top five things that you have implemented (along with the differences that they have made) from the previous five books you have read.

1. ....
....
....
....

2. ....
....
....
....

3. ....
....
....
....

4. ....
....
....
....

5. ....
....
....

51 TITLE: ....

AUTHOR: ....

ABOUT THE BOOK: ....
....
....
....
....
....

DESIGN & LAYOUT: ★★★★★

READABILITY: ★★★★★

QUALITY OF INFO: ★★★★★

FAVE QUOTE(S): ....
....
....
....
....
....
....
....

READING NOTES: ....
....
....
....
....
....
....
....
....
....
....

KEY TAKEAWAYS & THINGS TO IMPLEMENT: ....
....
....
....
....
....
....
....
....
....
....
....
....
....

52

TITLE: ....

AUTHOR: ....

ABOUT THE BOOK: ....
....
....
....
....
....
....

DESIGN & LAYOUT: ★ ★ ★ ★ ★

READABILITY: ★ ★ ★ ★ ★

QUALITY OF INFO: ★ ★ ★ ★ ★

FAVE QUOTE(S): ....
....
....
....
....
....
....
....

READING NOTES: ....

....

....

....

....

....

....

....

....

....

....

KEY TAKEAWAYS & THINGS TO IMPLEMENT: ....

....

....

....

....

....

....

....

....

....

....

....

53

TITLE: ....

AUTHOR: ....

ABOUT THE BOOK: ....
....
....
....
....
....

DESIGN & LAYOUT: ★ ★ ★ ★ ★

READABILITY: ★ ★ ★ ★ ★

QUALITY OF INFO: ★ ★ ★ ★ ★

FAVE QUOTE(S): ....
....
....
....
....
....
....
....

READING NOTES: ....
....
....
....
....
....
....
....
....
....

KEY TAKEAWAYS & THINGS TO IMPLEMENT: ....
....
....
....
....
....
....
....
....
....
....
....

54

TITLE: ....

AUTHOR: ....

ABOUT THE BOOK: ....
....
....
....
....
....

DESIGN & LAYOUT: ★ ★ ★ ★ ★

READABILITY: ★ ★ ★ ★ ★

QUALITY OF INFO: ★ ★ ★ ★ ★

FAVE QUOTE(S): ....
....
....
....
....
....
....
....

READING NOTES: ....

....

....

....

....

....

....

....

....

....

KEY TAKEAWAYS & THINGS TO IMPLEMENT: ....

....

....

....

....

....

....

....

....

....

....

55

TITLE: ....

AUTHOR: ....

ABOUT THE BOOK: ....
....
....
....
....
....

DESIGN & LAYOUT: ★★★★★

READABILITY: ★★★★★

QUALITY OF INFO: ★★★★★

FAVE QUOTE(S): ....
....
....
....
....
....
....
....

READING NOTES: ....

....

....

....

....

....

....

....

....

....

KEY TAKEAWAYS & THINGS TO IMPLEMENT: ....

....

....

....

....

....

....

....

....

....

....

"We are all in the gutter, but some of us are looking at the stars."

OSCAR WILDE

TOP 5 THINGS IMPLEMENTED

To help you stay focused on putting what you have learned into practice, list the top five things that you have implemented (along with the differences that they have made) from the previous five books you have read.

1. ....
....
....
....

2. ....
....
....
....

3. ....
....
....
....

4. ....
....
....
....

5. ....
....
....
....

56

TITLE: ....

AUTHOR: ....

ABOUT THE BOOK: ....
....
....
....
....
....

DESIGN & LAYOUT: ⭐⭐⭐⭐⭐

READABILITY: ⭐⭐⭐⭐⭐

QUALITY OF INFO: ⭐⭐⭐⭐⭐

FAVE QUOTE(S): ....
....
....
....
....
....
....
....

READING NOTES: ....
....
....
....
....
....
....
....
....
....
....

KEY TAKEAWAYS & THINGS TO IMPLEMENT: ....
....
....
....
....
....
....
....
....
....
....
....

57

TITLE: ....

AUTHOR: ....

ABOUT THE BOOK: ....
....
....
....
....
....

DESIGN & LAYOUT: ★★★★★

READABILITY: ★★★★★

QUALITY OF INFO: ★★★★★

FAVE QUOTE(S): ....
....
....
....
....
....
....
....

READING NOTES: ....
....
....
....
....
....
....
....
....
....

KEY TAKEAWAYS & THINGS TO IMPLEMENT: ....
....
....
....
....
....
....
....
....
....
....

TITLE: ....

AUTHOR: ....

ABOUT THE BOOK: ....
....
....
....
....
....

DESIGN & LAYOUT: ★ ★ ★ ★ ★

READABILITY: ★ ★ ★ ★ ★

QUALITY OF INFO: ★ ★ ★ ★ ★

FAVE QUOTE(S): ....
....
....
....
....
....
....
....

READING NOTES: ....

....

....

....

....

....

....

....

....

....

KEY TAKEAWAYS & THINGS TO IMPLEMENT: ....

....

....

....

....

....

....

....

....

....

....

59

TITLE: ....

AUTHOR: ....

ABOUT THE BOOK: ....
....
....
....
....
....

DESIGN & LAYOUT: ★★★★★

READABILITY: ★★★★★

QUALITY OF INFO: ★★★★★

FAVE QUOTE(S): ....
....
....
....
....
....
....
....

READING NOTES: ....
....
....
....
....
....
....
....
....
....

KEY TAKEAWAYS & THINGS TO IMPLEMENT: ....
....
....
....
....
....
....
....
....
....
....

60

TITLE: ....

AUTHOR: ....

ABOUT THE BOOK: ....
....
....
....
....
....

DESIGN & LAYOUT: ★★★★★

READABILITY: ★★★★★

QUALITY OF INFO: ★★★★★

FAVE QUOTE(S): ....
....
....
....
....
....
....
....

READING NOTES: ....
....
....
....
....
....
....
....
....
....
....

KEY TAKEAWAYS & THINGS TO IMPLEMENT: ....
....
....
....
....
....
....
....
....
....
....
....

"Personal development is the belief
that you are worth the effort,
time and energy needed to
develop yourself."

DENIS WAITLEY

TOP 5 THINGS IMPLEMENTED

To help you stay focused on putting what you have learned into practice, list the top five things that you have implemented (along with the differences that they have made) from the previous five books you have read.

1. ....
....
....
....

2. ....
....
....
....

3. ....
....
....
....

4. ....
....
....
....

5. ....
....
....
....

61

TITLE: ....

AUTHOR: ....

ABOUT THE BOOK: ....
....
....
....
....
....

DESIGN & LAYOUT: ★ ★ ★ ★ ★

READABILITY: ★ ★ ★ ★ ★

QUALITY OF INFO: ★ ★ ★ ★ ★

FAVE QUOTE(S): ....
....
....
....
....
....
....
....

READING NOTES: ....
....
....
....
....
....
....
....
....
....
....

KEY TAKEAWAYS & THINGS TO IMPLEMENT: ....
....
....
....
....
....
....
....
....
....
....
....

62

TITLE: ....

AUTHOR: ....

ABOUT THE BOOK: ....
....
....
....
....
....

DESIGN & LAYOUT: ☆ ☆ ☆ ☆ ☆

READABILITY: ☆ ☆ ☆ ☆ ☆

QUALITY OF INFO: ☆ ☆ ☆ ☆ ☆

FAVE QUOTE(S): ....
....
....
....
....
....
....
....

READING NOTES: ....

....

....

....

....

....

....

....

....

....

KEY TAKEAWAYS & THINGS TO IMPLEMENT: ....

....

....

....

....

....

....

....

....

....

....

63

TITLE: ....

AUTHOR: ....

ABOUT THE BOOK: ....
....
....
....
....
....

DESIGN & LAYOUT: ★ ★ ★ ★ ★

READABILITY: ★ ★ ★ ★ ★

QUALITY OF INFO: ★ ★ ★ ★ ★

FAVE QUOTE(S): ....
....
....
....
....
....
....
....

READING NOTES: ....

....

....

....

....

....

....

....

....

....

KEY TAKEAWAYS & THINGS TO IMPLEMENT: ....

....

....

....

....

....

....

....

....

....

....

....

64

TITLE: ....

AUTHOR: ....

ABOUT THE BOOK: ....
....
....
....
....
....

DESIGN & LAYOUT: ★★★★★

READABILITY: ★★★★★

QUALITY OF INFO: ★★★★★

FAVE QUOTE(S): ....
....
....
....
....
....
....
....

READING NOTES: ....
....
....
....
....
....
....
....
....
....

KEY TAKEAWAYS & THINGS TO IMPLEMENT: ....
....
....
....
....
....
....
....
....
....
....

65

TITLE: ....

AUTHOR: ....

ABOUT THE BOOK: ....
....
....
....
....
....

DESIGN & LAYOUT: ★★★★★

READABILITY: ★★★★★

QUALITY OF INFO: ★★★★★

FAVE QUOTE(S): ....
....
....
....
....
....
....
....

READING NOTES: ....
....
....
....
....
....
....
....
....
....

KEY TAKEAWAYS & THINGS TO IMPLEMENT: ....
....
....
....
....
....
....
....
....
....

"The more you read, the more things you will know. The more things that you learn, the more places you'll go."

DR. SEUSS

TOP 5 THINGS IMPLEMENTED

To help you stay focused on putting what you have learned into practice, list the top five things that you have implemented (along with the differences that they have made) from the previous five books you have read.

1. ....
....
....
....

2. ....
....
....
....

3. ....
....
....
....

4. ....
....
....
....

5. ....
....
....
....

66

TITLE: ....

AUTHOR: ....

ABOUT THE BOOK: ....
....
....
....
....
....

DESIGN & LAYOUT: ☆ ☆ ☆ ☆ ☆

READABILITY: ☆ ☆ ☆ ☆ ☆

QUALITY OF INFO: ☆ ☆ ☆ ☆ ☆

FAVE QUOTE(S): ....
....
....
....
....
....
....
....

READING NOTES: ....

....

....

....

....

....

....

....

....

....

KEY TAKEAWAYS & THINGS TO IMPLEMENT: ....

....

....

....

....

....

....

....

....

....

....

....

67

TITLE: ....

AUTHOR: ....

ABOUT THE BOOK: ....
....
....
....
....
....

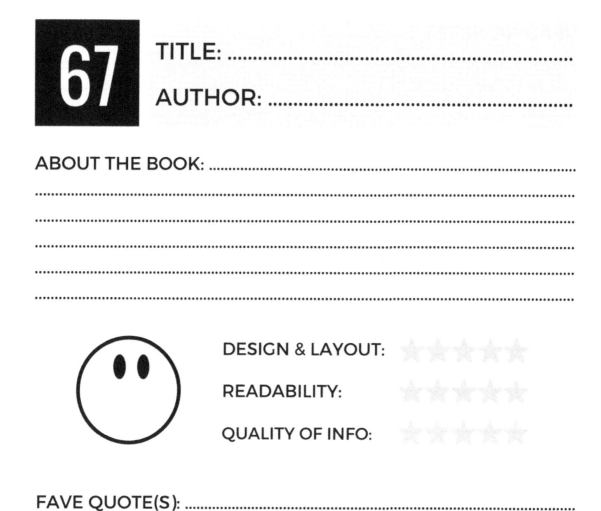

DESIGN & LAYOUT: ★★★★★

READABILITY: ★★★★★

QUALITY OF INFO: ★★★★★

FAVE QUOTE(S): ....
....
....
....
....
....
....
....
....

READING NOTES: ....
....
....
....
....
....
....
....
....
....

KEY TAKEAWAYS & THINGS TO IMPLEMENT: ....
....
....
....
....
....
....
....
....
....
....

68

TITLE: ....

AUTHOR: ....

ABOUT THE BOOK: ....
....
....
....
....
....

DESIGN & LAYOUT: ★★★★★

READABILITY: ★★★★★

QUALITY OF INFO: ★★★★★

FAVE QUOTE(S): ....
....
....
....
....
....
....
....

READING NOTES: ....

....

....

....

....

....

....

....

....

....

KEY TAKEAWAYS & THINGS TO IMPLEMENT: ....

....

....

....

....

....

....

....

....

....

....

....

69

TITLE: ....

AUTHOR: ....

ABOUT THE BOOK: ....
....
....
....
....
....

DESIGN & LAYOUT: ★ ★ ★ ★ ★

READABILITY: ★ ★ ★ ★ ★

QUALITY OF INFO: ★ ★ ★ ★ ★

FAVE QUOTE(S): ....
....
....
....
....
....
....
....

READING NOTES: ....

....

....

....

....

....

....

....

....

....

KEY TAKEAWAYS & THINGS TO IMPLEMENT: ....

....

....

....

....

....

....

....

....

....

....

....

70

TITLE: ....

AUTHOR: ....

ABOUT THE BOOK: ....
....
....
....
....
....

DESIGN & LAYOUT: ★ ★ ★ ★ ★

READABILITY: ★ ★ ★ ★ ★

QUALITY OF INFO: ★ ★ ★ ★ ★

FAVE QUOTE(S): ....
....
....
....
....
....
....
....

READING NOTES: ....

....

....

....

....

....

....

....

....

....

KEY TAKEAWAYS & THINGS TO IMPLEMENT: ....

....

....

....

....

....

....

....

....

....

....

....

....

"It's wise to keep in mind that neither success nor failure is ever final."

ROGER BABSON

TOP 5 THINGS IMPLEMENTED

To help you stay focused on putting what you have learned into practice, list the top five things that you have implemented (along with the differences that they have made) from the previous five books you have read.

1. ....
....
....
....

2. ....
....
....
....

3. ....
....
....
....

4. ....
....
....
....

5. ....
....
....
....

71

TITLE: ....

AUTHOR: ....

ABOUT THE BOOK: ....

....

....

....

....

....

DESIGN & LAYOUT: ★ ★ ★ ★ ★

READABILITY: ★ ★ ★ ★ ★

QUALITY OF INFO: ★ ★ ★ ★ ★

FAVE QUOTE(S): ....

....

....

....

....

....

....

....

....

READING NOTES: ....

....

....

....

....

....

....

....

....

....

KEY TAKEAWAYS & THINGS TO IMPLEMENT: ....

....

....

....

....

....

....

....

....

....

....

72

TITLE: ....

AUTHOR: ....

ABOUT THE BOOK: ....
....
....
....
....
....

DESIGN & LAYOUT: ★★★★★

READABILITY: ★★★★★

QUALITY OF INFO: ★★★★★

FAVE QUOTE(S): ....
....
....
....
....
....
....
....

READING NOTES: ....
....
....
....
....
....
....
....
....
....

KEY TAKEAWAYS & THINGS TO IMPLEMENT: ....
....
....
....
....
....
....
....
....
....
....

73   TITLE: ....

AUTHOR: ....

ABOUT THE BOOK: ....

....

....

....

....

....

DESIGN & LAYOUT: ★ ★ ★ ★ ★

READABILITY: ★ ★ ★ ★ ★

QUALITY OF INFO: ★ ★ ★ ★ ★

FAVE QUOTE(S): ....

....

....

....

....

....

....

....

....

READING NOTES: ....

....

....

....

....

....

....

....

....

....

KEY TAKEAWAYS & THINGS TO IMPLEMENT: ....

....

....

....

....

....

....

....

....

....

....

....

....

74

TITLE: ....

AUTHOR: ....

ABOUT THE BOOK: ....
....
....
....
....
....

DESIGN & LAYOUT: ⭐⭐⭐⭐⭐

READABILITY: ⭐⭐⭐⭐⭐

QUALITY OF INFO: ⭐⭐⭐⭐⭐

FAVE QUOTE(S): ....
....
....
....
....
....
....
....

READING NOTES: ....

....

....

....

....

....

....

....

....

....

KEY TAKEAWAYS & THINGS TO IMPLEMENT: ....

....

....

....

....

....

....

....

....

....

....

75

TITLE: ....

AUTHOR: ....

ABOUT THE BOOK: ....
....
....
....
....
....

DESIGN & LAYOUT: ⭐⭐⭐⭐⭐

READABILITY: ⭐⭐⭐⭐⭐

QUALITY OF INFO: ⭐⭐⭐⭐⭐

FAVE QUOTE(S): ....
....
....
....
....
....
....
....

READING NOTES: ....

....

....

....

....

....

....

....

....

....

KEY TAKEAWAYS & THINGS TO IMPLEMENT: ....

....

....

....

....

....

....

....

....

....

....

"The biggest temptation is to settle for too little."

THOMAS MERTON

TOP 5 THINGS IMPLEMENTED

To help you stay focused on putting what you have learned into practice, list the top five things that you have implemented (along with the differences that they have made) from the previous five books you have read.

1. ....
....
....
....

2. ....
....
....
....

3. ....
....
....
....

4. ....
....
....
....

5. ....
....
....
....

76

TITLE: ....

AUTHOR: ....

ABOUT THE BOOK: ....
....
....
....
....
....

DESIGN & LAYOUT: ★ ★ ★ ★ ★

READABILITY: ★ ★ ★ ★ ★

QUALITY OF INFO: ★ ★ ★ ★ ★

FAVE QUOTE(S): ....
....
....
....
....
....
....
....

READING NOTES: ....

....

....

....

....

....

....

....

....

....

KEY TAKEAWAYS & THINGS TO IMPLEMENT: ....

....

....

....

....

....

....

....

....

....

....

77

TITLE: ....

AUTHOR: ....

ABOUT THE BOOK: ....
....
....
....
....
....

DESIGN & LAYOUT: ⭐⭐⭐⭐⭐

READABILITY: ⭐⭐⭐⭐⭐

QUALITY OF INFO: ⭐⭐⭐⭐⭐

FAVE QUOTE(S): ....
....
....
....
....
....
....
....

READING NOTES: ....
....
....
....
....
....
....
....
....
....

KEY TAKEAWAYS & THINGS TO IMPLEMENT: ....
....
....
....
....
....
....
....
....
....
....
....

78

TITLE: ....

AUTHOR: ....

ABOUT THE BOOK: ....
....
....
....
....
....

DESIGN & LAYOUT: ★ ★ ★ ★ ★

READABILITY: ★ ★ ★ ★ ★

QUALITY OF INFO: ★ ★ ★ ★ ★

FAVE QUOTE(S): ....
....
....
....
....
....
....
....

READING NOTES: ....
....
....
....
....
....
....
....
....
....

KEY TAKEAWAYS & THINGS TO IMPLEMENT: ....
....
....
....
....
....
....
....
....
....
....

79

TITLE: ....

AUTHOR: ....

ABOUT THE BOOK: ....
....
....
....
....
....

DESIGN & LAYOUT: ★ ★ ★ ★ ★

READABILITY: ★ ★ ★ ★ ★

QUALITY OF INFO: ★ ★ ★ ★ ★

FAVE QUOTE(S): ....
....
....
....
....
....
....
....

READING NOTES: ....

....

....

....

....

....

....

....

....

....

....

KEY TAKEAWAYS & THINGS TO IMPLEMENT: ....

....

....

....

....

....

....

....

....

....

....

80

TITLE: ....

AUTHOR: ....

ABOUT THE BOOK: ....
....
....
....
....
....

DESIGN & LAYOUT: ★ ★ ★ ★ ★

READABILITY: ★ ★ ★ ★ ★

QUALITY OF INFO: ★ ★ ★ ★ ★

FAVE QUOTE(S): ....
....
....
....
....
....
....
....

READING NOTES: ....
....
....
....
....
....
....
....
....
....

KEY TAKEAWAYS & THINGS TO IMPLEMENT: ....
....
....
....
....
....
....
....
....
....
....
....

"It is the small decisions you and I make every single day that create our destiny."

TONY ROBBINS

TOP 5 THINGS IMPLEMENTED

To help you stay focused on putting what you have learned into practice, list the top five things that you have implemented (along with the differences that they have made) from the previous five books you have read.

1. ....
....
....
....

2. ....
....
....
....

3. ....
....
....
....

4. ....
....
....
....

5. ....
....
....
....

81

TITLE: ....

AUTHOR: ....

ABOUT THE BOOK: ....
....
....
....
....
....

DESIGN & LAYOUT: ⭐⭐⭐⭐⭐

READABILITY: ⭐⭐⭐⭐⭐

QUALITY OF INFO: ⭐⭐⭐⭐⭐

FAVE QUOTE(S): ....
....
....
....
....
....
....
....
....

READING NOTES: ....

....

....

....

....

....

....

....

....

....

KEY TAKEAWAYS & THINGS TO IMPLEMENT: ....

....

....

....

....

....

....

....

....

....

....

....

82

TITLE: ....

AUTHOR: ....

ABOUT THE BOOK: ....
....
....
....
....
....

DESIGN & LAYOUT: ★ ★ ★ ★ ★

READABILITY: ★ ★ ★ ★ ★

QUALITY OF INFO: ★ ★ ★ ★ ★

FAVE QUOTE(S): ....
....
....
....
....
....
....
....

READING NOTES: ....
....
....
....
....
....
....
....
....
....
....

KEY TAKEAWAYS & THINGS TO IMPLEMENT: ....
....
....
....
....
....
....
....
....
....
....
....
....

83

TITLE: ....

AUTHOR: ....

ABOUT THE BOOK: ....
....
....
....
....
....

DESIGN & LAYOUT: ★★★★★

READABILITY: ★★★★★

QUALITY OF INFO: ★★★★★

FAVE QUOTE(S): ....
....
....
....
....
....
....
....

READING NOTES: ....
....
....
....
....
....
....
....
....
....

KEY TAKEAWAYS & THINGS TO IMPLEMENT: ....
....
....
....
....
....
....
....
....
....
....
....

84

TITLE: ....

AUTHOR: ....

ABOUT THE BOOK: ....
....
....
....
....
....

DESIGN & LAYOUT: ★ ★ ★ ★ ★

READABILITY: ★ ★ ★ ★ ★

QUALITY OF INFO: ★ ★ ★ ★ ★

FAVE QUOTE(S): ....
....
....
....
....
....
....
....

READING NOTES: ....
....
....
....
....
....
....
....
....
....
....

KEY TAKEAWAYS & THINGS TO IMPLEMENT: ....
....
....
....
....
....
....
....
....
....
....

85 TITLE: ....

AUTHOR: ....

ABOUT THE BOOK: ....
....
....
....
....
....

DESIGN & LAYOUT: ★★★★★

READABILITY: ★★★★★

QUALITY OF INFO: ★★★★★

FAVE QUOTE(S): ....
....
....
....
....
....
....
....

READING NOTES: ....

....

....

....

....

....

....

....

....

....

KEY TAKEAWAYS & THINGS TO IMPLEMENT: ....

....

....

....

....

....

....

....

....

....

....

....

....

"The bad news is time flies.
The good news is you're the pilot."

MICHAEL ALTSHULER

TOP 5 THINGS IMPLEMENTED

To help you stay focused on putting what you have learned into practice, list the top five things that you have implemented (along with the differences that they have made) from the previous five books you have read.

1. ....
....
....
....

2. ....
....
....
....

3. ....
....
....
....

4. ....
....
....
....

5. ....
....
....
....

86

TITLE: ....

AUTHOR: ....

ABOUT THE BOOK: ....
....
....
....
....
....

DESIGN & LAYOUT: ⭐ ⭐ ⭐ ⭐ ⭐

READABILITY: ⭐ ⭐ ⭐ ⭐ ⭐

QUALITY OF INFO: ⭐ ⭐ ⭐ ⭐ ⭐

FAVE QUOTE(S): ....
....
....
....
....
....
....
....

READING NOTES: ....

....

....

....

....

....

....

....

....

....

KEY TAKEAWAYS & THINGS TO IMPLEMENT: ....

....

....

....

....

....

....

....

....

....

....

87 TITLE: ....

AUTHOR: ....

ABOUT THE BOOK: ....
....
....
....
....
....

DESIGN & LAYOUT: ★★★★★

READABILITY: ★★★★★

QUALITY OF INFO: ★★★★★

FAVE QUOTE(S): ....
....
....
....
....
....
....
....

READING NOTES: ....
....
....
....
....
....
....
....
....
....

KEY TAKEAWAYS & THINGS TO IMPLEMENT: ....
....
....
....
....
....
....
....
....
....
....
....

88

TITLE: ....

AUTHOR: ....

ABOUT THE BOOK: ....
....
....
....
....
....

DESIGN & LAYOUT: ★ ★ ★ ★ ★

READABILITY: ★ ★ ★ ★ ★

QUALITY OF INFO: ★ ★ ★ ★ ★

FAVE QUOTE(S): ....
....
....
....
....
....
....
....

READING NOTES: ....

....

....

....

....

....

....

....

....

....

KEY TAKEAWAYS & THINGS TO IMPLEMENT: ....

....

....

....

....

....

....

....

....

....

....

....

89

TITLE: ....

AUTHOR: ....

ABOUT THE BOOK: ....
....
....
....
....
....

DESIGN & LAYOUT: ★ ★ ★ ★ ★

READABILITY: ★ ★ ★ ★ ★

QUALITY OF INFO: ★ ★ ★ ★ ★

FAVE QUOTE(S): ....
....
....
....
....
....
....
....

READING NOTES: ....
....
....
....
....
....
....
....
....
....

KEY TAKEAWAYS & THINGS TO IMPLEMENT: ....
....
....
....
....
....
....
....
....
....
....
....

90

TITLE: ....

AUTHOR: ....

ABOUT THE BOOK: ....
....
....
....
....
....

DESIGN & LAYOUT: ★★★★★

READABILITY: ★★★★★

QUALITY OF INFO: ★★★★★

FAVE QUOTE(S): ....
....
....
....
....
....
....
....

READING NOTES: ....
....
....
....
....
....
....
....
....
....

KEY TAKEAWAYS & THINGS TO IMPLEMENT: ....
....
....
....
....
....
....
....
....
....
....

"What would you attempt to do if you knew you would not fail?"

ROBERT SCHULLER

TOP 5 THINGS IMPLEMENTED

To help you stay focused on putting what you have learned into practice, list the top five things that you have implemented (along with the differences that they have made) from the previous five books you have read.

1. ....
....
....
....

2. ....
....
....
....

3. ....
....
....
....

4. ....
....
....
....

5. ....
....
....
....

91

TITLE: ....

AUTHOR: ....

ABOUT THE BOOK: ....
....
....
....
....
....

DESIGN & LAYOUT: ★ ★ ★ ★ ★

READABILITY: ★ ★ ★ ★ ★

QUALITY OF INFO: ★ ★ ★ ★ ★

FAVE QUOTE(S): ....
....
....
....
....
....
....
....

READING NOTES: ....

....

....

....

....

....

....

....

....

....

KEY TAKEAWAYS & THINGS TO IMPLEMENT: ....

....

....

....

....

....

....

....

....

....

....

....

92

TITLE: ....

AUTHOR: ....

ABOUT THE BOOK: ....
....
....
....
....
....

DESIGN & LAYOUT: ⭐⭐⭐⭐⭐

READABILITY: ⭐⭐⭐⭐⭐

QUALITY OF INFO: ⭐⭐⭐⭐⭐

FAVE QUOTE(S): ....
....
....
....
....
....
....
....

READING NOTES: ....

....
....
....
....
....
....
....
....
....

KEY TAKEAWAYS & THINGS TO IMPLEMENT: ....

....
....
....
....
....
....
....
....
....
....
....
....

93

TITLE: ....

AUTHOR: ....

ABOUT THE BOOK: ....
....
....
....
....
....

DESIGN & LAYOUT: ★ ★ ★ ★ ★

READABILITY: ★ ★ ★ ★ ★

QUALITY OF INFO: ★ ★ ★ ★ ★

FAVE QUOTE(S): ....
....
....
....
....
....
....
....

READING NOTES: ....

....

....

....

....

....

....

....

....

....

KEY TAKEAWAYS & THINGS TO IMPLEMENT: ....

....

....

....

....

....

....

....

....

....

....

....

94

TITLE: ....

AUTHOR: ....

ABOUT THE BOOK: ....

....
....
....
....
....

DESIGN & LAYOUT: ★ ★ ★ ★ ★

READABILITY: ★ ★ ★ ★ ★

QUALITY OF INFO: ★ ★ ★ ★ ★

FAVE QUOTE(S): ....

....
....
....
....
....
....
....
....

READING NOTES: ....
....
....
....
....
....
....
....
....
....

KEY TAKEAWAYS & THINGS TO IMPLEMENT: ....
....
....
....
....
....
....
....
....
....
....
....

95

TITLE: ....

AUTHOR: ....

ABOUT THE BOOK: ....
....
....
....
....
....

DESIGN & LAYOUT: ★ ★ ★ ★ ★

READABILITY: ★ ★ ★ ★ ★

QUALITY OF INFO: ★ ★ ★ ★ ★

FAVE QUOTE(S): ....
....
....
....
....
....
....
....

READING NOTES: ....

....

....

....

....

....

....

....

....

....

KEY TAKEAWAYS & THINGS TO IMPLEMENT: ....

....

....

....

....

....

....

....

....

....

....

....

*"Those at the top of the mountain
didn't fall there."*

MARCUS WASHLING

TOP 5 THINGS IMPLEMENTED

To help you stay focused on putting what you have learned into practice, list the top five things that you have implemented (along with the differences that they have made) from the previous five books you have read.

1. ....
....
....
....

2. ....
....
....
....

3. ....
....
....
....

4. ....
....
....
....

5. ....
....
....
....

96

TITLE: ....

AUTHOR: ....

ABOUT THE BOOK: ....
....
....
....
....
....

DESIGN & LAYOUT: ★★★★★

READABILITY: ★★★★★

QUALITY OF INFO: ★★★★★

FAVE QUOTE(S): ....
....
....
....
....
....
....
....

READING NOTES: ....

....

....

....

....

....

....

....

....

....

KEY TAKEAWAYS & THINGS TO IMPLEMENT: ....

....

....

....

....

....

....

....

....

....

....

....

97

TITLE: ....

AUTHOR: ....

ABOUT THE BOOK: ....
....
....
....
....
....

DESIGN & LAYOUT: ★★★★★

READABILITY: ★★★★★

QUALITY OF INFO: ★★★★★

FAVE QUOTE(S): ....
....
....
....
....
....
....
....

READING NOTES: ....

....

....

....

....

....

....

....

....

....

KEY TAKEAWAYS & THINGS TO IMPLEMENT: ....

....

....

....

....

....

....

....

....

....

....

....

98

TITLE: ....

AUTHOR: ....

ABOUT THE BOOK: ....
....
....
....
....
....

DESIGN & LAYOUT: ★ ★ ★ ★ ★

READABILITY: ★ ★ ★ ★ ★

QUALITY OF INFO: ★ ★ ★ ★ ★

FAVE QUOTE(S): ....
....
....
....
....
....
....
....

READING NOTES: ....

....

....

....

....

....

....

....

....

....

....

KEY TAKEAWAYS & THINGS TO IMPLEMENT: ....

....

....

....

....

....

....

....

....

....

....

....

....

99

TITLE: ....

AUTHOR: ....

ABOUT THE BOOK: ....
....
....
....
....
....

DESIGN & LAYOUT: ⭐⭐⭐⭐⭐

READABILITY: ⭐⭐⭐⭐⭐

QUALITY OF INFO: ⭐⭐⭐⭐⭐

FAVE QUOTE(S): ....
....
....
....
....
....
....
....

READING NOTES: ....
....
....
....
....
....
....
....
....
....
....

KEY TAKEAWAYS & THINGS TO IMPLEMENT: ....
....
....
....
....
....
....
....
....
....
....
....

100

TITLE: ....

AUTHOR: ....

ABOUT THE BOOK: ....
....
....
....
....
....

DESIGN & LAYOUT: ★ ★ ★ ★ ★

READABILITY: ★ ★ ★ ★ ★

QUALITY OF INFO: ★ ★ ★ ★ ★

FAVE QUOTE(S): ....
....
....
....
....
....
....
....

READING NOTES: ....

....
....
....
....
....
....
....
....
....
....

KEY TAKEAWAYS & THINGS TO IMPLEMENT: ....

....
....
....
....
....
....
....
....
....
....
....

"The successful man will profit from his mistakes and try again in a different way."

DALE CARNEGIE

TOP 5 THINGS IMPLEMENTED

To help you stay focused on putting what you have learned into practice, list the top five things that you have implemented (along with the differences that they have made) from the previous five books you have read.

1. ....
....
....
....

2. ....
....
....
....

3. ....
....
....
....

4. ....
....
....
....

5. ....
....
....
....

A LITTLE ABOUT ME...

At the beginning of 2017, I started a YouTube channel and blog dedicated to reviewing non-fiction books in the categories of business, entrepreneurship, marketing, and personal development.

Up until that point, you could count the number of books that I had read from front to back on one hand!

I hated reading.

But when I discovered that there is an undeniable link between those that continually invest in themselves through reading and those that are successful, I knew I had to up my game.

My YouTube channel and blog became my motivation for reading - if I was going to review a lot of books, then I had to read a lot of books.

A little over a year later, I can now say that I am an avid reader and I am reaping the benefits from the additional knowledge that I have gained.

I created these worksheets to help me keep track of the books that I had read and to help keep me focused on implementing what I learned along the way. Since they worked so well for me, I thought I would share them with you, hence, My Book of 100 Books was (self-)published.

I hope that you have found this book useful in achieving your goals.

Roseanna

BLOG: BookReviews.RoseannaSunley.com
INSTAGRAM: @RoseannaSunleyBooks
FACEBOOK: @RoseannaSunleyBooks
TWITTER: @RoseannaBooks
YOUTUBE: Roseanna Sunley - Business Book Reviews

I enjoy connecting with other non-fiction book lovers, sharing key takeaways, and hearing about other recommended reads.

Made in the USA
Monee, IL
09 September 2021